Do not lose hope in Allah's mercy.

Do not lose hope in Allah's mercy.
(39:53)

Allah knows every whisper of the soul.

Call upon Me; I will respond to you.
(40:60)

Righteous deeds will be rewarded, regardless of gender.
(4:124)

Allah
will test you,
so be patient.
(2:155)

Allah is with you
wherever you are.
(57:4)

Allah is closer than
your jugular vein.
(50:16)

Allah is the
most merciful.
(7:151)

Do not lose
hope in
Allah's mercy.
(39:53)

Allah knows every whisper of the soul.
(50:16)

The Quran is
made easy
to remember.
(54:17)

ALLAH FOUND YOU
LOST
AND GUIDED YOU.
(93:7)

Women also have a
share in inheritance.
(4:7)

Speak kindly to people and uphold your commitments.
(2:83)

You may dislike
something that
is good for you.
(4:19)

Call upon Me,
I will respond
to you.
(40:60)

Righteous deeds will
be rewarded,
regardless of gender.
(4:124)

Every small good deed counts.
(99:7)

With hardship
comes ease.
(94:6)

Rely on Allah
after making
a decision.
(3:159)

Believers will
triumph
through faith.
(3:139)

He created life
and death
to test you.
(67:2)

Prayer prevents immorality and wrongdoing.
(29:45)

Homes are
places of rest.
(16:80)

Muhammad
was sent as
mercy to the worlds.
(21:107)

Allah is with you
wherever you are.
(57:4)

Believing women should be modest.
(24:31)

Allah will test you, so be patient.
(2:155)

Every small act of
good will be seen.
(99:7)

The Quran guides
to the best path.
(17:9)

Remember Me, and
I will remember you.
(2:152)

Do not lose hope
or be sad.
(3:139)

Allah is the most merciful.
(7:151)

Allah wishes to
lighten
your burdens.
(4:28)

Allah will give you, and you will be satisfied.
(93:5)

Recognize
Allah's grace.
(27:40)

Allah made night
and day
for reflection.
(25:62)

Allah is closer than your jugular vein.
(50:16)

(27:73)

Don't let hatred
make you unjust.
(5:8)

Say,
'My Lord,
increase my
knowledge.
(20:114)

Worldly life is a
delusional enjoyment.
(3:185)

Humans are created
in the best form.
(95:4)

So whoever does
an atom's weight
of good will see it.
(99:7)

Believers who do good
will be guided
by their faith.
(10:9)

Treat parents well.
(29:8)

Hasten to forgiveness from your Lord.
(3:133)

Feed the needy,
orphan,
and captive.
(76:8)

Your ally is
Allah
and His
Messenger.
(5:55)

Hold firmly
to Allah's rope.
(3:103)

Allah does not burden a soul beyond that it can bear.
(2:286)

Forgetting
Allah leads
to self
forgetfulness.
(59:19)

Listen to the Quran
for mercy.
(7:204)

The Hereafter
is better
than this life.
(93:4)

Allah
will provide a
way out for those
who fear Him.
(65:2)

Strivers in faith
will be guided.
(29:69)

Allah won't
change a people
unless
they change
themselves.
(13:11)

Allah eases the
affairs of the
God-fearing.
(65:4)

www.ingramcontent.com/pod-product-compliance
Lightning Source LLC
La Vergne TN
LVHW061940070526
838199LV00060B/3892
9789198927528